ARTIST TRANSCRIPTIONS

AL Di MEOLA • JOHN McLAU

M000234279

FRIDAY NIGHT IN SAN FRANCISCO

65 Fantasia Suite

48 Frevo Rasgado

86 Guardian Angel

3 Mediterranean Sundance/Rio Ancho

29 Short Tales Of The Black Forest

21st CENTURY MUSIC PRODUCTIONS

EXCLUSIVELY DISTRIBUTED BY

HAL•LEONARD™ CORPORATION

7777 W. BLUEMOUND RD. P.O. BOX 13819 MILWAUKEE, WI 53213

ISBN 978-0-7935-1246-1

Mediterranean Sundance / Rio Ancho

Music by Al Di Meola and Paco DeLucia

4

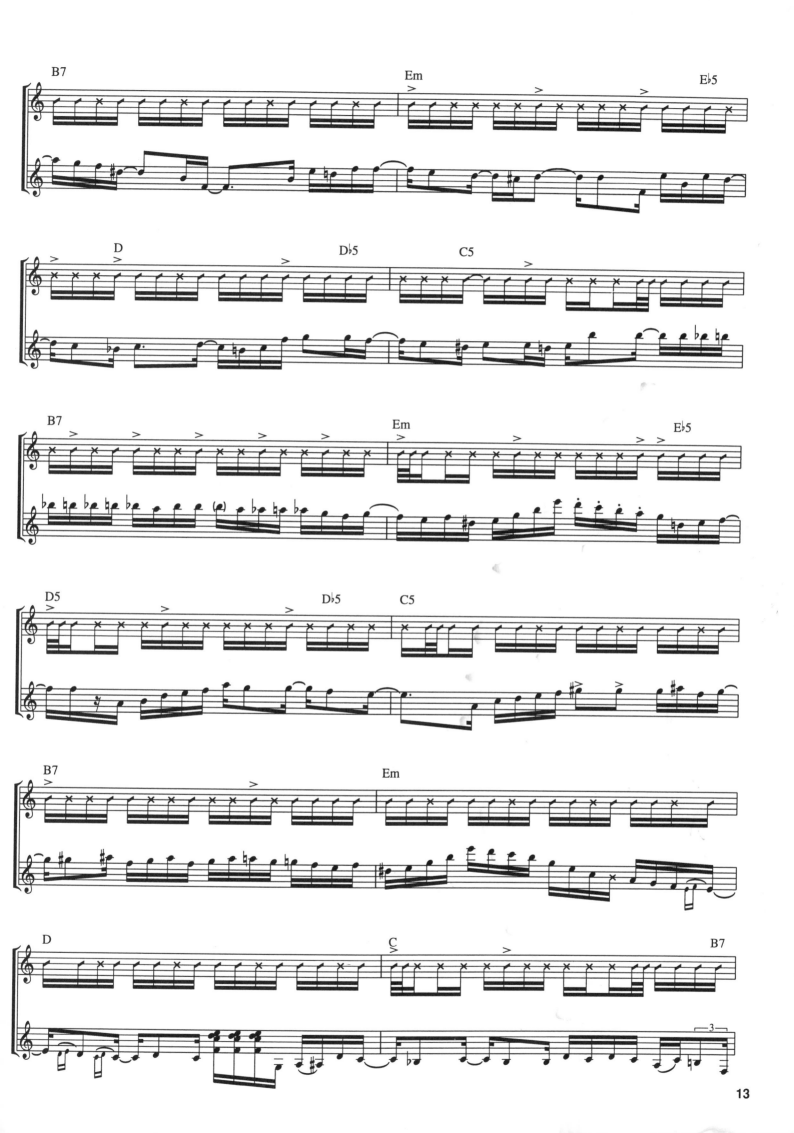

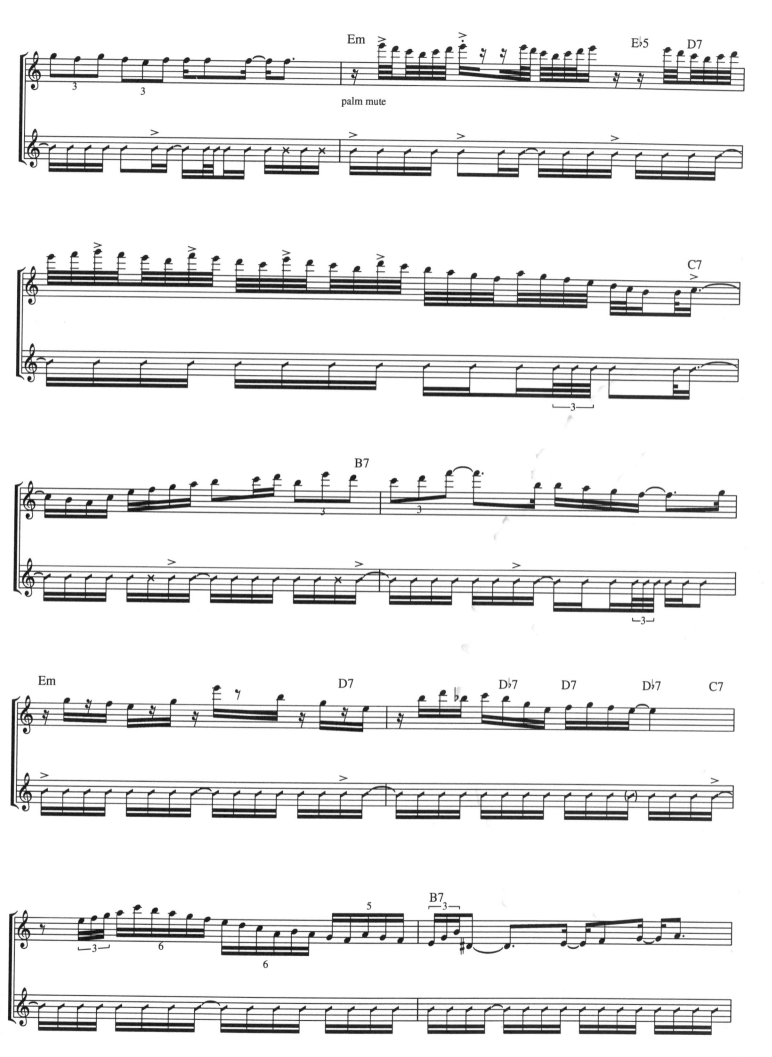

22

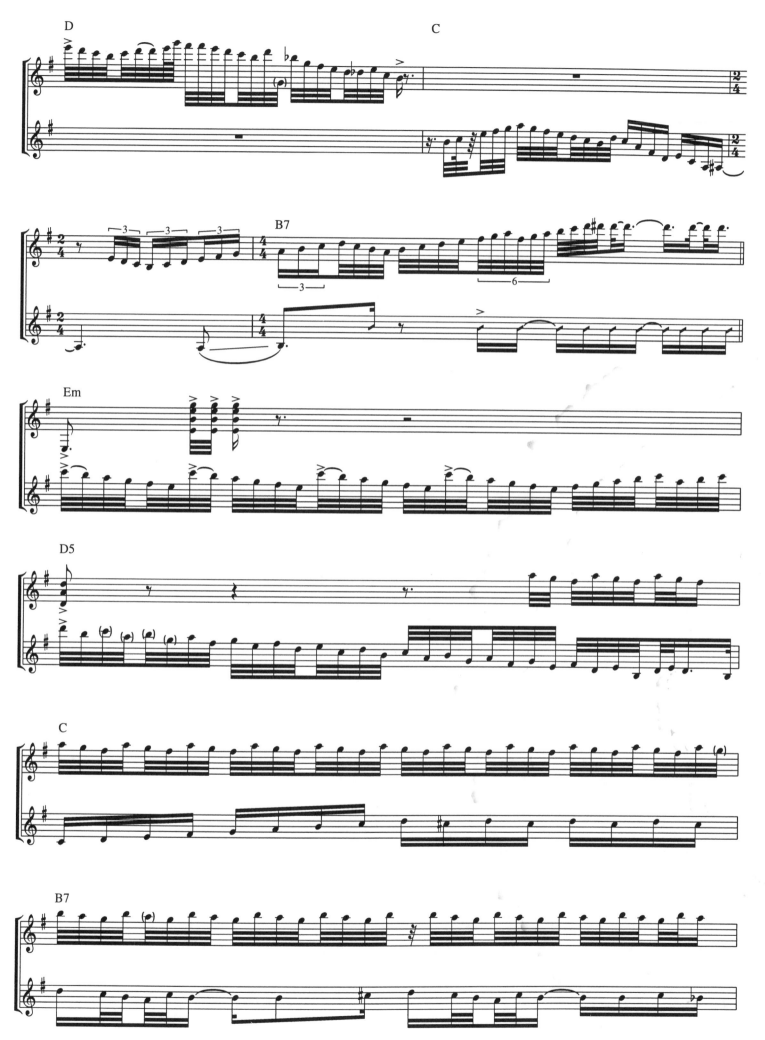

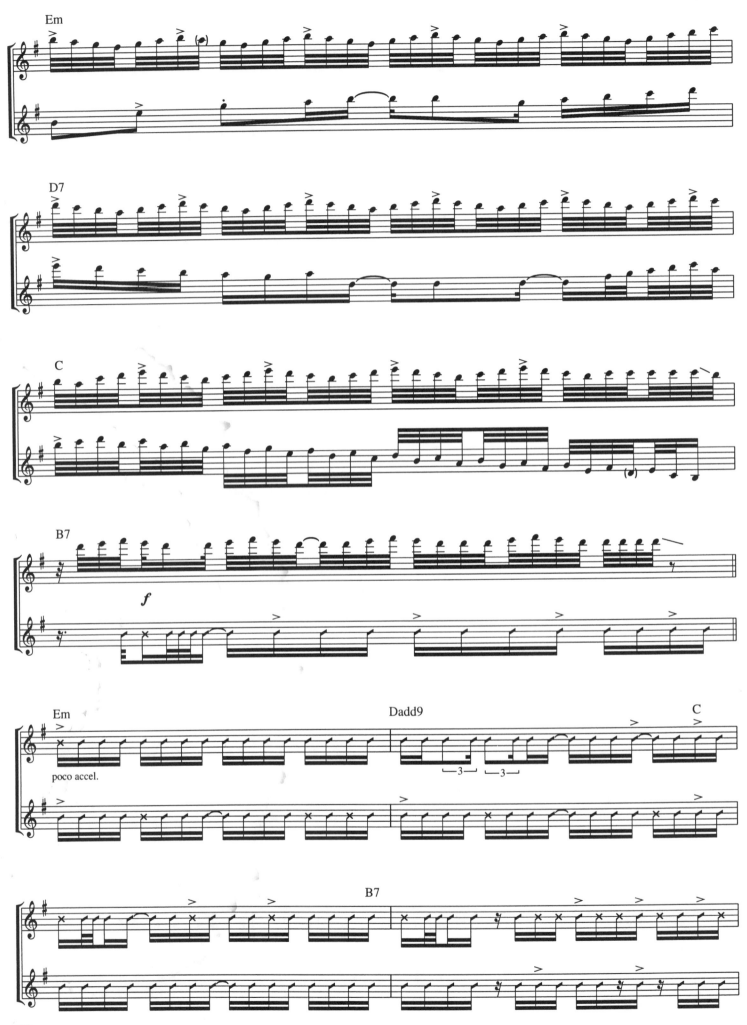

Short Tales Of The Black Forest

By Chick Corea

Slap guitar body

on cue:

cresc.

Poco accel .

Poco accel .

Poco accel.

P.M.

Scrape strings

F G A

F G A B♭ A G A B♭ A G   F G A

This trill spans 4 frets and rises and falls in a roughly chromatic sequence, starting and shifting at these pitches.

slap guitar body

F5   G5   A5

Asus4

D

Asus4

D

6

Frevo Rasgado

Music by Egberto Gismonti

Fine

Fantasia Suite

By Al Di Meola

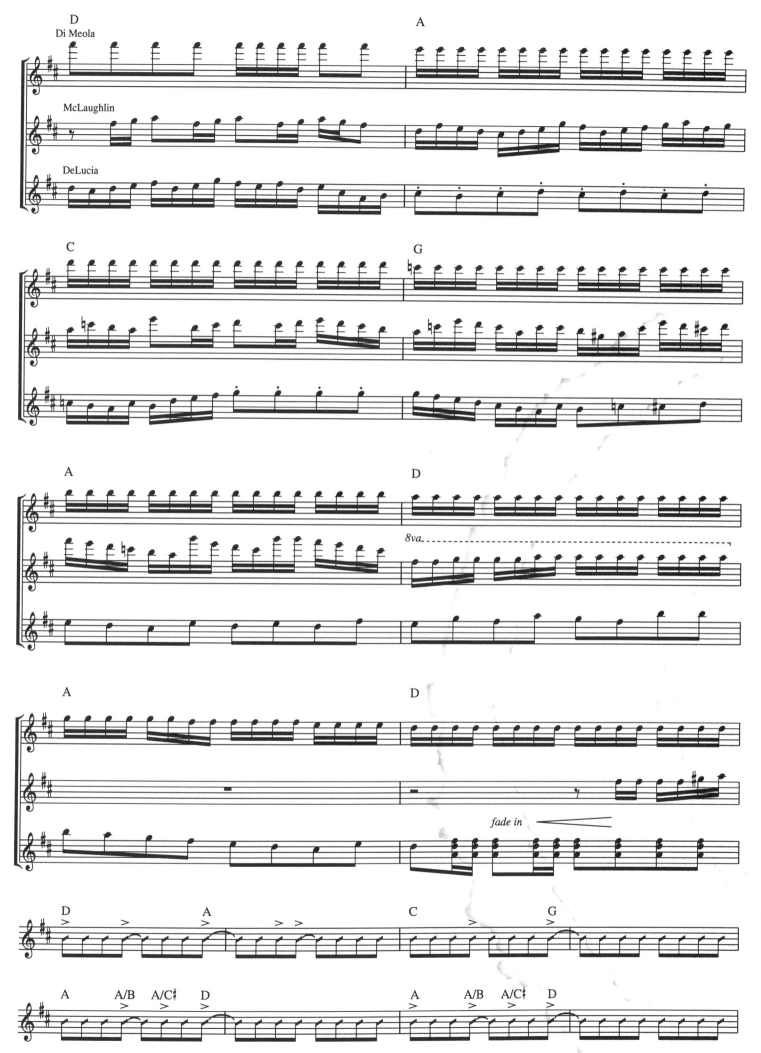

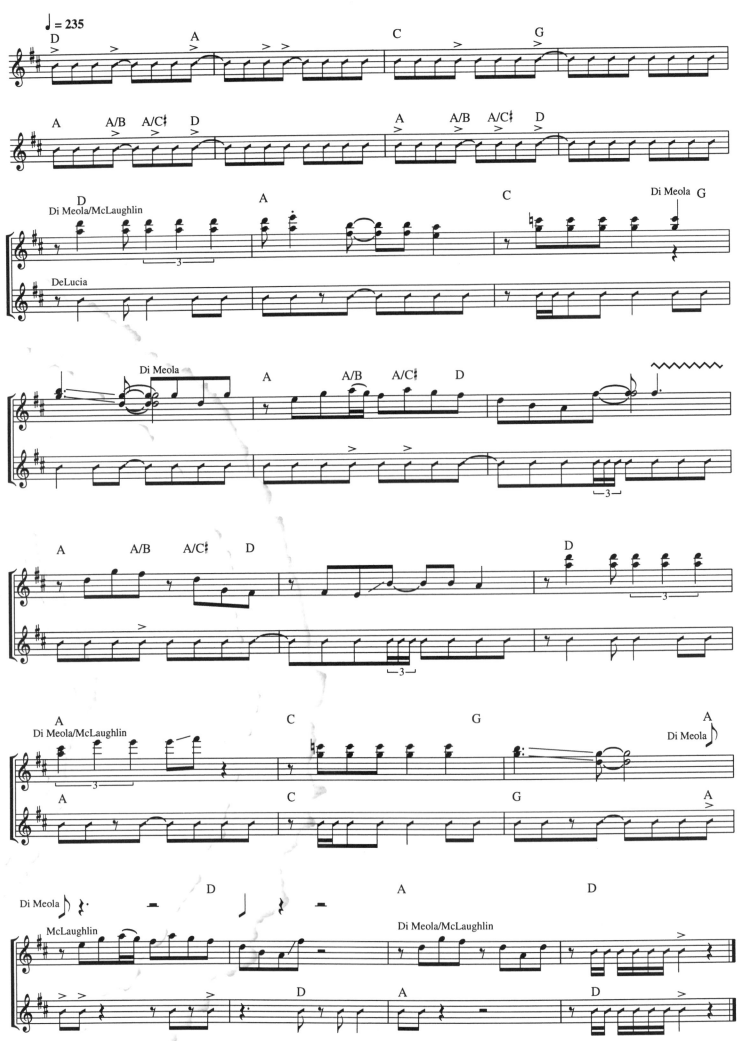

Guardian Angel

by John McLaughlin

McLaughlin

Di Meola

DeLucia

B Em

D

C7

F

Am

G

C   C

B7